Domes · Cliffs · and Waterfalls

... A Brief Geology of Yosemite Valley

by
William R. Jones

YOSEMITE
ASSOCIATION

Yosemite National Park, California

ISBN 0-939666-05-7

ACKNOWLEDGEMENTS: Assisting were King Huber and Dallas Peck
of the U.S. Geological Survey, Henry Berrey of the Yosemite Association,
and Leonard McKenzie of the National Park Service.
Based on an earlier work by M.E. Beatty. Drawings by B. Weiss.
Photos courtesy of the National Park Service.

 *Printed on recycled paper*

Introduction...an Historic Puzzle

What a puzzle Yosemite Valley was to those who first saw the marvelous gorge! Early Miwok Indians imagined rocks that grew and people turned to stone. A pioneer reported a cliff that looked sliced, like a loaf of bread.

Josiah Whitney explained the scene in 1865 with his "bottom-dropping-out" theory: Half Dome had been "split asunder, the lost half having gone down in the wreck of matter and the crush of worlds." Next came John Muir. To Muir the bottom had never fallen out of anything God had made, and he set about to answer "How did the Lord make it? What tools did He use? How did He apply them and when?" Soon Muir had his answer, advising others on how to find it: "Patient observation and constant brooding above the rocks, lying upon them for years as the ice did, is the way to arrive at the truths which are graven so lavishly upon them." Professor Whitney thought the glacier theory "absurd", and called Muir a "mere sheepherder" (which he was) and an "ignoramus".

And so it went until 1913 when twelve theories existed explaining the valley's origin. Then Francois Matthes began work, mapping and studying, and in 1930 came out for Muir. Since then, observation, debate, and refinement have gone on.

This brief geology, then, is the up-to-date refinement of over a century of study to understand this world's unique valley. Why are these roundest domes, sheerest cliffs, and finest waterfalls here?

El Capitan...bold granite

El Capitan means "The Chief," and it is — the tallest unbroken cliff in the world. Fully 3,000 feet high, it is tough granite rock.

Yosemite Valley has several kinds of granite, with many variations. Most of the major kinds are named for spectacular cliffs or rock formations that they compose. Of these granites, that named for El Capitan resists weathering most strongly. Because of this, the El Capitan granite almost closes in the valley's outlet area. Too, in the lower part of the valley where this granite's El Capitan and Cathedral Rock masses project from opposite walls, El Capitan granite constricts the valley again. The El Capitan scenic formation is not made purely of El Capitan granite, however. Its summit brow is Taft granite, and about halfway up the cliff face darker diorites shape a "map of North America."

Mineral grains of Yosemite's granites are formed so well and are of such a size that they must have crystallized without interference and over a long period, as from a hot fluid deep within the insulating earth. This origin gave them a relatively large grain size, and hence a resistance to fracturing.

El Capitan granite was the first of the Valley granites to form, about 108 million years ago. After solidifying at least partly, the mass cracked. Some cracks penetrated to still-molten zones. Liquid rock flowed along the new fissures into outer areas, solidifying there and thus "healing" the cracks as though with mortar.

Silica also helps rocks resist weathering, and El Capitan granite has a high proportion. At places in the valley where rocks have less silica or more cracks, the valley walls are at most hackled cliffs in retreat. Below such spots lie immense piles of rock rubble, fallen from their parent cliffs above. An example is the Rockslides, just down valley from El Capitan below a diorite having both finer cracks and a lower silica content.

In the time since the granites formed, streams and glaciers wore into them, trimming away the weakest rocks the most, to carve out Yosemite Valley. But the bold "Rock Chief," formed of the toughest granite of all, they left.

THREE BROTHERS...FORMATION IN TRIPLICATE

Compared to rocks at many places, Yosemite Valley's granites have few cracks, and often these few are spaced widely and extend great distances, cleaving the granites boldly. Frequently the cracks (or "joints") are in a parallel set, and sometimes there are 2 or more such sets that intersect. Such a pattern occurs in the midsection of Yosemite Valley, with the finest expression of this characteristic in the Three Brothers. In this rock formation, three sloping "roofs" rise one above another, each pitched at the same angle and truncated by equally regular vertical cliffs. Across the valley from this point are similar asymmetric spurs; and their roofs, slanting steps, and gables can be connected by sight with those of the Three Brothers. The same three intersecting joint sets guide all these forms.

Such master fractures occur over much of Yosemite National Park. Often they cross directly over scenic formations and rock types, sometimes for miles, showing up strongly at places and poorly at others. This trait of continuity is a clue that these master cracks formed after most or all of the granites had solidified. Stresses on the grand scale, probably from the rise of the Sierra Nevada itself, caused these widespread features.

Streams always follow the course of least resistance, and thus they often are guided by strong fractures. In the midvalley south of the Three Brothers, for instance, one streamlet cuts downward obliquely along a slanted joint plane. It slides sideways against one canyon wall, cutting an overhang, rather than eroding downward vertically.

Water enters the joints initially in small quantities, weathering the rock's fresh crystals into loosened grains that wash or blow away, broadening the original tiny cracks. Such cracks at The Fissures, originally too narrow for a knife-blade to enter, are now gaping abysses too wide to stride.

Glaciers can carry off bigger blocks. The glaciers that flowed through Yosemite Valley nearly overtopped the Three Brothers, pressing against its slopes. Deep within, the ice quarried away large chunks along planes of weakness parallel to the great faces, exposing the strong inner cores and leaving an architectural whole — in triplicate.

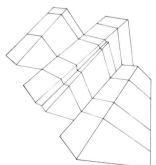

Royal Arches and North Dome...geologic sisters

Granite is the rock that forms domes best, but of the several granite varieties in Yosemite Valley, only two make impressive domes. The granite named for Half Dome makes up the walls and rims at the valley head, including Half Dome, North Dome, Basket Dome, Liberty Cap, Mount Broderick, Mount Starr King, Mount Watkins, and several lesser domes. El Capitan granite makes up the walls and rims in parts of the middle and lower valley, including Sentinel Dome, El Capitan, and Turtleback Dome.

The story of the domes, thus, begins with the story of the granites. That is deep within the earth, 87 million years ago for the domes association with Half Dome, 108 million years ago for those with El Capitan. When these molten rocks crystallized into granites, they were perhaps as much as five miles below the earth's surface.

You can imagine the pressure beneath water that deep. Triple this for rock, nearly three times as heavy. Such was the pressure on the Yosemite granites when they formed. Now, uplifted and with the miles of overburden once above them removed by erosion, they are at the surface. Only the air is upon them. However, their internal pressure remains. Normally this rock pressure releases along the myriad of close cracks that develop as erosion exposes rocks to lower pressure. But these two Yosemite granites have developed few internal cracks, and so in them the pressure pushing outward breaks new cracks under their sur-

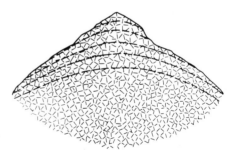

faces. Over time, layers pop loose from the host rock, smoothing its surfaces and allowing longer, curving cracks to generate underneath. The result is that still more massive layers "exfoliate", with even bigger scales or "leaves" falling away. And so the outer zones of the granite outcrops begin to resemble the concentric layers of an onion, like North Dome. The Royal Arches below the dome, with exfoliation slabs up to 200 feet thick, show the process in cross-section.

You may have seen other kinds of exfoliation. Rocks around a campfire expand from the heat and may break off in big flakes. Wetting of a rock by rain or spray causes its mica minerals to expand, and this pressure, too, causes the outside rock layers to separate. These kinds of exfoliation produce only small-scale effects, easier to see than that of load relief responsible for massive domes. But exfoliation by load relief is as active as these other kinds — plates continue to warp outward on the baldrock exposures about Yosemite Valley. Its domes are forming still!

Half Dome...and its other "half"

Domes are rare in the world. To have one with a part so cleanly missing is stranger still. Half Dome, symbol of Yosemite, has no counterpart. Was it once Whole Dome?

The granite rock that makes up Half Dome (and that is named for this famous feature) occurs as bedrock over a wide surrounding region. Half Dome's frontal cliff is indeed the remaining side of a great cracked block of granite! This cliff aligns with a series of long cracks through the earth here, part of a system of internal block structure prevalent throughout the rest of Yosemite and the entire Sierra Nevada mountain range. The same system, but in finer fractures, also is seen in the shoulder to the left of the Half Dome cliff.

On a nearby ridge above this shoulder, a mountaineer can find a boulder foreign to its resting place, an "erratic". This boulder

had to be deposited there so high above today's streams by a glacier that brought it down from the High Sierra. The boulder tells us that the ice sea, when deepest, covered all but the top 700 feet of Half Dome's 4,800 foot height above Yosemite Valley. The dome's rounded summit, therefore, is not a glacial feature but another product of exfoliation. In fact, this upper part of the dome has probably been standing much as it is today for millions of years — before, during, and since the Ice Age — its strength making it nearly impervious to time's effects.

Now it should be easy to imagine the glacier flowing slowly but persistently past the elongate dome, beginning to transfigure the mass to its shape today — quarrying away block after block along the dome's one weak zone of vertical cracks, but elsewhere where the rock was firm only smoothing and polishing. Later, smaller glaciers nestled under the cliff itself, probably steepened it still further as they eroded backward against it.

Still, where did the other part (not half, probably only a small fraction) go? The glacier carried some pieces down below what is now the floor of Yosemite Valley, and they are now buried there. It dumped other parts at its snout, until floodwaters sluiced this debris downcanyon to the San Joaquin Valley. There, on that valley plain far to the west, lie pieces of rock just like that in and around Half Dome. And if present patterns continue, someday all of Half Dome will be there, or in the ocean beyond.

470 MILLION YEARS IN THE YOSEMITE VALLEY REGION
THE STORY STARTS HERE...

1 470 to 220 million years ago — Layered sediments blanket the seafloor adjacent to the western North American continent.

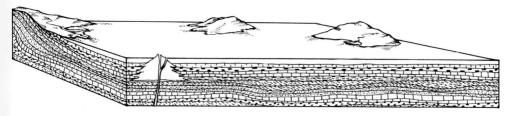

2 220 to 80 million years ago — Masses of molten rock rise from below. Fluid off-shoots break out at the surface to form volcanoes. The covering sedimentary and volcanic rocks crumple into folds, their higher strata rising above sea level, and then into an ancestral Sierra Nevada mountain range.

3 80 to 25 million years ago — Erosion strips away most of the old sedimentary and volcanic rocks in the Yosemite region, exposing the former molten masses now cooled to granite rock.

4 25 million years ago — A rolling surface of rounded low hills and broad valleys — including the primordial Yosemite Valley — has developed. The Merced River meanders, yet to cut 3,000 feet into the rock to reach its present position.

7 2 million years ago — The Ice Age begins. During it, glaciers from the High Sierra nearly fill Yosemite Valley with their massive ice, widening its stream canyon and steepening the walls where waterfalls will leap once the ice melts.

8 20,000 years ago — The last glacier to enter Yosemite Valley passes just downcanyon beyond El Capitan and Bridalveil Fall, leaving a moraine ridge at its snout.

BRIDALVEIL FALL...A "HANGING" VALLEY

To a person looking up from the floor of Yosemite Valley, Bridalveil Fall seems to drop over a wall directly from the sky. Behind the clifftop, however, is a valley leading up to a rolling plateau.

Usually sidestreams join their trunkstream at its same level. Those that do not are in "hanging valleys," a phrase particularly descriptive of the source of Bridalveil Fall, for it hangs 620 feet above the Yosemite Valley floor. (Yosemite Falls' valley hangs 2,425 feet!)

How did this come to be?

The Sierra Nevada has not always existed as a mountain range. Before it did, there was only a sea. Some 220 million years ago, the sediments on the bottom of this sea began rising, although not continuously. One especially long pause in the rise of this great block of the earth's crust lasted from 80 until 25 million years ago. During that time streams evened off the block's surface. (This is the surface now above Yosemite Valley; it has changed slightly since.)

When lifting resumed, the eastern edge of the Sierra block rose faster than the western. Main streams flowing down the tilting slope quickened. One of these, the ancestral Merced River, cut downward into its broad and low primordial Yosemite Valley. Meanwhile the Merced River's Bridalveil Creek sidestream, flowing more nearly across the tilting block, was steepened less and could erode little more than before. So the Merced River left the Bridalveil Creek valley stranded above, with the creek tumbling from there down Yosemite Valley's side to join its master stream.

Now the Ice Age began. At intervals for two million years, glaciers followed down the pre-existing stream valleys, filling them to their brims. The ice eroded downward into Yosemite Valley and also trimmed the walls back, widening the valley. Earlier glaciers accomplished the most, and by 700,000 years ago when those massive ice bodies melted, Bridalveil Creek was uncovered, its former cascading mouth dropping even more steeply to the Merced River.

In the time since, spray has billowed against the Fall's cliff, wetting it especially near the bottom. Moisture has penetrated the mica grains of the granite there, expanding them until layers of rock have broken loose to fall away, leaving a growing recess at the waterfall's base. Today the mouth of Bridalveil Creek is steeper still than when the melting glacier first revealed it. It now drops in true waterfall fashion.

This history is true not only for Bridalveil Fall, but also for Yosemite Falls, Sentinel Falls, and Ribbon Fall — all on similar sidestreams off the Merced River. Nevada and Vernal Falls, on the main trunkstream flowing down the range, take another story, however.

6 10 to 2 million years ago — Further uplift continues steepening the Merced River; now the river cuts a deeper canyon.

10 Today — The Lake basin has filled. Meadows and forested flats serve as a base for millions of park visitors to admire the scene.

5 25 to 10 million years ago — Renewed uplift of the Sierra Nevada steepens the Merced River, causing the river to cut into its former broad valley.

9 10,000 years ago — Behind the glacier's moraine ridge in the basin scooped out by the ice, the last Ancient Lake Yosemite fills with meltwater. (Earlier glaciers also formed lakes.) Streams from the receding ice dump sediment into the lake, building deltas.

VERNAL AND NEVADA FALLS...GIANT STAIRWAY

Linking the head of Yosemite Valley with Little Yosemite Valley above are the two imposing steps of the Giant Stairway. Directly in the path of the Merced River, they force that stream to tumble in fine waterfalls. Vernal Fall (the closer one) is 317 feet high, Nevada Fall is 594 feet.

Notice the cliffs over which the falls drop. They are at a right angle to each other, and each cliff is parallel to one of the two master fracture patterns that occur throughout the Sierra Nevada. The cliff at Nevada Fall (the upper fall) is also parallel to the cliff face of Half Dome.

Notice, too, that the steps are much broader than the stream. They are canyonwide steps. The glaciers that coursed from the High Sierra down this gorge rasped at the granite, trimming away rock on the downcanyon sides of the fracture planes, leaving a lowered tread below each. These eroded zones may have been where the bedrock had cracked more. They also could have been the sites of earlier soil-filled depressions when chemical weathering dominated. Either or both conditions explain how the glaciers excavated just portions of the stairway, leaving the tough rocks of the giant steps for the waterfalls to drop over.

If the removal of so much granite rock is hard to imagine, note that the ice was thick here. Only the highest land in this scene stood above the glacier. Even Liberty Cap (the high rock dome to the left of Nevada Fall) was covered by 1,000 feet.

Glaciers accentuate irregularities in their channels. They erode with vigor where their ice is thickest. Where depressions occur in their beds, they descend into these with a plunging motion and press heavily on the weaker rock there that initially caused the depression. Where projections caused by resistant rocks occur, glaciers flow horizontally or even upslope, minimizing erosive force. Where rocks are truly obdurate, then, such erosional favoritism makes them stand out even more, as they do in the extreme in the Nevada and Vernal Falls cliffs, intact relics from the Ice Age.

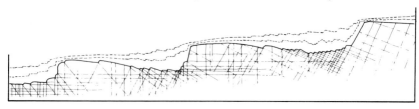

THE VALLEY FLOOR...ANCIENT LAKE BED

Here is perhaps the strangest feature of all for a rugged valley in a bold mountain range — a flat floor. Seven miles long and about half a mile wide, this floor has level forested flats, lush meadows, sand beaches, and a meandering river with deep quiet pools.

When glaciers flowed through Yosemite Valley, they found the rock in the central part slightly weaker than at the head of the valley or at the outlet. That two trunk glaciers converged here in their flow down the range must also have contributed to the valley's erosion. And so the ice gouged downward, excavating a basin as deep as 2,000 feet below the present floor (5,000 feet or more below the rims), but rising at the lower end of the valley to carry debris up over the bedrock lip there and then on down the canyon. Probably most digging was as early as one million years ago, by earlier large glaciers. After the ice melted, the first Lake Yosemite formed in its abandoned bed, finally filling with sediment and rock. Later glaciers dug into this loose material in their turn, although less deeply, and also left similar lakes.

The first glacier stopped in the lower valley not far below Bridalveil Fall, at Bridalveil Meadow. There, because the glacier had been carrying rock and because of bulldoz-ing action by its thin snout that pushed ahead as stiff ice, this glacier built a series of rubble ridges. Behind these the ice melted again, forming the last of the lakes in the valley. This lake was nearly five miles long, its waters at first milky white with finely ground rock ("glacial flour"), then pale green, and finally blue, reflecting the magnificent scenic formations of the valley, doubling their beauty.

This lake did not last, either. In the 15,000 or so years since its birth, the last Ancient Lake Yosemite basin has also filled in. The

Merced River brought pebbles and sand down the canyon to the head of the lake, dropped them in the still water, and slowly built a delta down the valley. Sidestreams built their deltas outward. Rocks fell in from the cliffs. Sediment finally filled the lake basin, and its waters were gone forever. Forests and meadows now stand on the former deltas.

Thus, the same glacial force that set the stage with domes, cliffs, and waterfalls built the platform from which to view its creations.

Mirror Lake...change

Ancient Lake Yosemite finally filled in with sediment, forming rootholds for sedges and willows, then meadow grasses and forest trees. We find clues for this at Mirror Lake, just above the head of Yosemite Valley in the Tenaya Canyon side-drainage. There the lake-filling process can be seen in action. Up this canyon is a mile-long flat, reminiscent of the Yosemite Valley floor, through which Tenaya Creek meanders to the relict Mirror Lake, dammed by a low rock ridge.

This site cannot be a remnant of Ancient Lake Yosemite, for the Tenaya Canyon flat is at a higher altitude than the Valley floor. Neither can Mirror Lake have been a glacial lake, for none of the rocks in the ridge across its outlet are like those up the canyon where the glacier came from. Instead, they are the same as the bedrock in the slopes of Half Dome and North Dome above the lake. It was from these cliffs, therefore, that the rocks came, falling perhaps during an earthquake or a sharp frost when ice expanding in a crack pressed them loose, to tumble into the canyon and block the little stream, backing it into the lake that has so magnificently reflected the sources of its creation. Thus, although the chasm in which this little lake sits once bore the mighty Tenaya Canyon glacier, the lake formed after the Ice Age.

Early visitors recall Mirror Lake being much larger, and it was. The lake probably would be gone now except that the natural dam across its outlet was built up by park managers in the 1800s to raise the water level. But geological processes are now prevailing here, and we may soon call this "Ancient Lake Mirror." Even now, late summer visitors often call it Mirror Meadow.

High Sierra...Source of Glaciers

During winter many feet of snow fall in Yosemite Valley. At an altitude of 4,000 feet above sea level, however, the valley is too warm in summer for the snow to remain. Yet we know that ice streams once nearly buried Half Dome, that the glacier was nearly a mile thick where it passed through Yosemite Valley, and that ice went downcanyon beyond to an altitude of less than 2,000 feet! Even during the Ice Age, glaciers could not form in the Yosemite region much below 8,000 feet. From where did the ice come?

In much of the United States, the ice that during the Ice Age plowed and furrowed as far south as Kansas came down from North America's continental ice cap. In the West, however, that cap did not extend south of Washington. Here in the Sierra Nevada, it happened that the range had risen to its full height just about the time the Ice Age began. The High Sierra caught the snow then as now, and, either because the climate was colder then or more snow fell (or both), the snow collected over the years rather than melt away. The broad Tuolumne Meadows, for instance, at 8,600 feet was a zone of snow accumulation. Even more ice flowed there from surrounding peaks.

Ice, of course, is brittle in small pieces or thin slabs. In these forms it will crack and break. At a thickness of a hundred feet or more, however, the lower layers are under such pressure that they glide away, downhill normally but in other directions if blocked ... And so in the Sierra Nevada the ice formed in the shadows of high mountain peaks flowed mainly down along the pre-existing stream valleys. It flowed slowly, any given point moving only a few tens of feet per day. Obviously such a slow rate would require great volume to move away the annual snowfall, and the glaciers were immensely thick.

The Ice Age had many glacial pulses. As the period waned, ice advances became shorter. Now we are experiencing one more ice advance, a minor one so far. The High Sierra peaks once again have glaciers. In the later 1800s, these ice masses were pushing actively against their end moraine ridges; but now they're only half as big as then, growing some years, shrinking most. So, is the Ice Age over? If not, what will Half Dome, Bridalveil Fall, and El Capitan look like after the next large glacier goes by?

OTHER YOSEMITES...

The word "yosemite" is sometimes used as a generic form denoting a type of valley similar in origin and appearance to Yosemite Valley. Several of these are in the Sierra Nevada — all at about the same place on the western slope, situated along westflowing master streams, carved from granite, and glaciated. Little Yosemite Valley, up the Merced River from its namesake, is the most obvious example. Just north on the Tuolumne River is Hetch Hetchy Valley (shown here), with waterfalls, a cliff like El Capitan, and a dome. To the south are Tehipite Canyon with a tall dome, and the open Kings River Canyon.

Other yosemites (although not necessarily carved from granite) are in other mountain chains — the Rocky Mountains, Alps, Himalayas, Andes — and in the sea level fjords of the north. Antarctica must have yosemites, too; perhaps under its ice a glacier is now making one that will surpass Yosemite itself.

MERCED CANYON...CLUE TO YOSEMITE VALLEY'S ORIGINAL V-SHAPE

Mountain streams characteristically cut canyons that are V-shaped in cross-section, and down from Yosemite Valley below the extent of its glaciers the Merced Canyon has that shape. Probably Yosemite Valley looked much the same as the Merced Canyon until glaciers trimmed out the bottom of Yosemite's V, widening it into the U-shape typical of glacial valleys.

OLDEST ROCKS...LAYERED STRATA

Yosemite Valley is now composed almost entirely of granites, but these were not the first rocks of this region. Instead, Yosemite's granites intrude still earlier oceanic sediments and volcanic rocks deposited here from 470 to 220 million years ago. These strata had been pressed so deeply into the hot earth that their mineral grains recrystallized. You can see remnants of these older "metamorphic" rocks on all the Yosemite approaches — Tioga, Big Oak Flat, Wawona, and Merced Roads. They are usually dark gray or red in color, and often still show their original sedimentary layers as bands, sometimes in contorted folds. A thin and discontinuous band of them trends north-south across Yosemite Valley in its midsection not far east of Sentinel Dome and Yosemite Falls.

Synthesizing the Story...The Yosemite Falls Example

Renewed uplift and westward tilting quickened the Merced River flowing down the Sierra slope, and this trunk stream wore deeply into its bed, carving a sloping-walled canyon 3,000 feet deep, predecessor to today's Yosemite Valley. Into this canyon, Yosemite Creek cascaded.

Two to one million years ago early glaciers began widening this V-shaped canyon into a U-shaped gorge. By 700,000 years ago, their cutting left Yosemite Creek hanging high above the valley floor, its former cascading connection with the Merced River steepened. Wetting from spray undercut the Creek's precipitous slope still more, and the waterfall leaps came to be.

The Upper Fall's leap ends just where a brushy ledge intersects its course; the Lower Fall's leap begins just where another ledge crosses. These are master fractures, nearly horizontal, in the otherwise sparsely-jointed granite, and they pre-determined there would be two Yosemite Falls and how each would look.

At the right of the Upper Fall, the great Yosemite Point cliff stands, slowly forming exfoliation slabs parallel to the surface due to the pressure from within. A freestanding sliver of one of these remains as the Lost Arrow.

Below, the Valley floor is flat, the Merced River meandering to receive the waters from Yosemite Creek, as the river and creek once joined in filling the ancient lake left there by the last glacier.

The scene is not static. The waterfalls steepen slightly as slabs fall from their bases, rocks fall from the cliffs to build piles below, and the river moves its load of sand shed from the granites through the valley and on to the sea.

Yosemite Falls drops into the valley as the star performer, especially in spring when air at the waterfall base throbs from the compression, reverberating up and down the valley. But the waterfall's stage was a long time in setting.

In several pulses between 220 and 80 million years ago, the granite rocks in view crystallized from a molten state deep within the earth. What was to become the Sierra Nevada was beginning its long rise from below the sea; a pause in this uplift from 80 to 25 million years ago allowed the streams to wear down the surface into a rolling plateau, across which Yosemite Creek still flows as it heads for the falls.